# SIMPLIFYING RETAIL

Either Re-invent your Retail concept or Perish....

RITESH MOHAN

BlueRose Publishers

First Published in October 2020

**ISBN:** 978-93-90396-04-7

**BLUEROSE PUBLISHERS**

www.bluerosepublishers.com

info@bluerosepublishers.com

+91 8882 898 898

**Cover Design:**

Mohit Joshi

**Typographic Design:**

Saurabh Yadav

**Distributed by:** BlueRose, Amazon, Flipkart, Shopclues

# Disclaimer

# Introduction

## Retail as defined by Wikipedia

Retail is the process of selling consumer goods or services to customers through multiple channels of distribution to earn a profit.

Retailers are basically service providers that fill small orders of a large number of individuals, who are the end-users or consumers.

Shopping generally refers to the act of buying products.

Retail markets and shops have a very ancient history, dating back to antiquity.

Shopping centers have greatly evolved since their inception in America's giant post war suburban boom. They have also moved from being perceived by consumers as having a special status in the 1950's and 1960's to a far more common place in the late twentieth century.

Over the centuries, retail shops were transformed from little shops to the sophisticated experiential destinations in the shopping malls of the modern era.

## Retail Evolution

Retail is one of the oldest sectors in any economy. It directly gets impacted with demand and supply fluctuations. Let us dive deep into retail evolution-

1950 – 1975: retail was dominated by single Mom & Pop shops located at the corner of the street, managed mainly by a family who used to stock daily groceries, fresh food items, meat etc. Shoppers made requests to the store owner at the counter which were fulfilled by the shop owner himself.

You would still find these type of shops mainly called Kiranas in India and they form a huge segment of unorganized retail sector in the Indian subcontinent.

1975-90: retail witnessed an era wherein organized retailing was seen; small corner side shops transformed by branding themselves and a few of them took a huge leap by turning into shopping centers. This was an era wherein a new generation of earlier single shop owners took charge of their business from their forefathers and equipped with a drive for expansion, they experimented with their shop concepts and gave it a human touch, wherein the shoppers could touch and feel the products that they needed.

This era also saw the rise of big retailers like Woolworths etc.

1990's to Current web 2.0: technology and web 2.0 completely revolutionized shoppers' habits with the introduction of e-commerce, which has contributed to the removal of international borders.

Technology has even enabled "regular" people to sell online on pure-player websites like Amazon, and Etsy. Technology has now enabled anyone to become a retailer using Marketplaces like Amazon etc.

Concepts like 'Buy Online', Pickup In Store (BOPIS) are giving birth to a new age of retailing. What's more, today's shoppers are all about "retailtainment": shopping is a leisure activity that they truly enjoy.

Omni-channel experiences are what consumers expect, and if you're not meeting their needs they'll go straight to your competitors- just like the retailers of old, who were not able to adapt in the past and failed.

Hence retail is not dying and will never die, it will simply evolve.

Retail apocalypse or Retail renaissance

Let's first of all understand that retail is not dying but bad retail is certainly dying. Brands which refuse to adapt themselves to changing consumer's buying behavior would vanish.

According to Forrester's latest research, the most successful retailers are the ones focused on using technology to become better retailers — *not* just better innovators.

Being first is not important but being fast in your actions determines your success in the new age economics.

The biggest challenge for any mall management or retail brand today, is to drive footfall in to their shops. The answer lies in digital receipts or e-receipts.

Digital receipts or E-receipts is the bi-product of Big data or Artificial intelligence and machine learning algorithms can offer some relief to the mall's dwindling footfalls and can help brands to revive their customer experience and also help retailers to fight against the retail apocalypse phenomenon.

## Premise of Digital receipts or E-receipts

### Personalized Communication

Thirty-five percent of the shoppers say they're more likely to purchase from a retailer that sends personalized advertising, and 36% want more customized experiences.

**Source:** Masters of the Top Four Retail Tech Trends

Your receipt or printed invoice holds tremendous potential of data analytics and customer insights and this forms the key basis or premise of digital receipts.

Digital receipts can now power up your digital marketing program like never before.

I shall now explain by presenting a case study as to how retail is evolving & new business models are thriving in this new age of retailing.

## Case study of brand using power of AI and Machine learning

**Brand:** Third love (lingerie online retailer)

This online retailer has built USD 750 Million business by exposing the weakness of Victoria's secret brand.

## How do they do it?

Third Love's big difference from the other start-ups, including True & Co. & Adore Me, is its use of voluminous amount of data—600 million data points such as breast shape, cup fit and band tightness from over 11 million women that it has culled from an online questionnaire—to create better-fitting bras, especially by pioneering the use of half-sizes.

Third Love acquired Indi Custom, an app that made custom jeans by taking measurements, in 2013, even before launching the first product.

They tweaked Indi's technology to focus on bra fit and created the Third Love app, which took two photos of users in their underwear or in form-fitting clothing to calculate body size and churn out a bra size recommendation.

The process was similar to how high-tech makers of custom suits and 3-D-printed shoes work their magic.

Customer friendly approach: For the cost of shipping, Third Love sends the customers a bra they can take the tags off of and wear for 30 days. If a customer doesn't like it, she can send it back for free.

Result: using technology & AI algorithms, Third love brand is today valued at USD 750 million and is still growing.

The aim of this book is to simplify retail management and encourage retailpreneurship amongst the millennial's. I have followed a pedagogy of using real life case studies to explain the concepts and strategy behind a brand's success.

We shall be covering topics relating to merchandising, key formulae and terminologies that you would need to know, sales management, retail operations, branding and finally leadership skills. Throughout the book, my approach would be presenting case studies and live examples in order to make the concept of retailing simpler.

# Table of Contents

# Chapter 1

## Know your matter

To excel in any industry and field, you need to know or at least be aware of the rules of the game and its important terms and formulae, so that you stay abreast when these terms are spoken about.

This chapter will teach you important ground rules and formulae which if followed regularly could sky-rocket your retail career.

### Average Inventory

This can be figured by taking an item price and subtracting discounts, plus freight and taxes.

The average is found by adding the beginning cost inventory for each month plus the ending cost inventory for the last month in the period.

### Here's a cost example-

If a clothing retailer has an average inventory of $100,000 and the cost of goods sold is $200,000, then you would divide $200,000 by $100,000 to give you a ratio of 2:1, which can be expressed simply as 2.

*Average Inventory (Month) = (Beginning of Month Inventory + End of Month Inventory) ÷ 2*

## Break-Even Analysis

This is the point in your retail business where sales equal expenses. There is no profit and no loss. For example, for a retail store, rent is likely to be the same regardless of the number of units sold.

*Break-Even ($) = Fixed Costs ÷ Gross Margin Percentage*

## Cost of Goods Sold

This is the price paid for a product, plus any additional costs necessary to get the merchandise into inventory and ready for sale, including shipping and handling. This method is pretty straight-forward, and very easy to use and implement in a low-volume, high-cost-per-item retail format.

## Gross Margin

This is simply the difference between what an item costs and the price for which it sells. For example, if Store A and B have the same sales, yet Store A's gross margin is 45 percent and Store B's gross margin is 55 percent, it's easy to see which store is faring better.

*Gross Margin = Total Sales - Cost of Goods*

## Gross Margin Return on Investment (GMROI)

GMROI calculations assist buyers in evaluating whether a sufficient gross margin is being earned by the products purchased, compared to the investment in inventory required to generate those gross margin dollars. For example, if your store has a sales volume of $2 million a year on an average inventory of $1million; that would be pretty good. But $2 million on an average inventory of $500,000 (though uncommon) would be even better.

*GMROI = Gross Margin $ ÷ Average Inventory Cost*

## Initial Markup

Initial markup (IMU) is a calculation to determine the selling price a retailer puts on an item in their store. There are factors like competition for like products, perceived value and initial mark downs that may affect initial markup settings.

## Inventory Turnover (Stock Turn)

Inventory turnover is the number of times during a certain calendar period; a retailer sells its inventory and replaces it.

*Turnover = Net Sales ÷ Average Retail Stock*

## Margin

This is the amount of gross profit a business earns when an item is sold. For example, if you have to pay $10 for each shirt and you then sell it to customers for $40, your retail margin equals $30.

*Margin % = (Retail Price - Cost) ÷ Retail Price*

## Net Sales

Net sales is the number of sales generated by a business after the deduction of returns, allowances for damaged or missing goods, and any discounts allowed.

*Net Sales = Gross Sales - Returns and Allowances*

## Open to Buy

Open to Buy (OTB) is the difference between the inventory needed and the inventory is available. That includes inventory on hand, in transit, and any outstanding orders. We shall understand this function in chapter 5 (what factors can make or break your retail business)

*OTB (retail) = Planned Sales + Planned Markdowns + Planned End of Month Inventory - Planned Beginning of Month Inventory*

## Sales per Square Foot

The sales per square foot data is most commonly used for planning inventory purchases. This data can also roughly calculate return on investment and is used to determine rent at a retail location.

*Sales per Square Foot = Total Net Sales ÷ Square Feet of Selling Space*

## Sell-Through Rate

This figure is a comparison of the amount of inventory a retailer receives from a manufacturer or supplier to what is actually sold. It is typically expressed as a percentage.

*Sell-Through % = Units Sold ÷ Units Received*

## Example:

During the month of June you sell 100 trousers. You received 200 trousers in receipts. You end June with 800 units of trousers of stock (End of Month Stock). What was your Beginning On-Hand units of trousers and what was your sell-through?

Beginning of Month stock (BOM) = EOM 800 units - Receipts 200 units + Sales 100 units = 700 units sell-through = sales 100 units / Beginning Inventory (BOM) 700 = 14.3% sell-through in June.

BOM means Beginning of Month

EOM means End of Month

Stock-to-Sales Ratio

Stock-to-sales ratio is the beginning-of-the-month-stock to the number of sales for the month. The key takeaway is that this ratio is a monthly metric.

*Stock-to-ales = Beginning of Month Stock ÷ Sales for the Month*

## Important retail metrics

### Sales per Square Foot

The sales per square foot data are most commonly used for planning inventory purchases. It can also roughly calculate return on investment and is used to determine rent for a retail location. Normally retailers, who do have a storage area within store, consider only the selling space area and ignore the storage area space; however, mostly retailers these days are taking the whole leased area space for carrying our sales per square foot.

*Sales per Square Foot of Selling Space = Total Net Sales ÷ Square Feet of Selling Space*

### Sales per Linear Foot of Shelf Space

A retail store with wall units and other shelf space may want to use sales per linear foot of shelf space to determine a product or product category's allotment of space.

*Sales per Linear Foot = Total Net Sales ÷ Linear Feet of Shelving*

## Sales by Department or Category

Retailers selling various categories of products will find the sales by department tool useful in comparing product categories within a store. For example, a men's clothing store can see how the sales of the accessories (ties & belts) department compare to the rest of the store's sales.

*Category's % of Total Store Sales = Category's Total Net Sales ÷ Store's Total Net Sales*

## Average ticket size

Also known as sales per customer, the sales per transaction number tells a retailer what is the average transaction in dollars.

*Sales per Transaction = Gross Sales ÷ Number of Transactions*

## Sales per Employee

This is the store sales generated by the number of store staffs present. This is an excellent tool for determining the number of sales a business needs to generate when increasing staffing levels.

*Sales per Employee = Net Sales ÷ Number of Employees*

## Retail financial metrics

These are the financial terms that are normally used in retail and it is important to know their values.

## Accounts Payable

It is the money owed to a creditor, generally an open account. It usually comprises of vendors or suppliers for your goods.

## Accounts Receivable

It os the sales of goods or services not yet collected. In other words, it's the money owed to you by your customer after they have taken possession of the goods or after you have delivered your services.

## Accrual Basis

It is one of the two types of accounting methods used (cash and accrual). When using accrual basis for your accounting, sales are reported on the income statement for the period (month) when they were earned (regardless of when it is collected), and expenses are reported in the period when they occur (regardless of when you paid the bill).

## Accrued Expenses

These are the expenses which have been incurred but have not been paid. An example would be payroll.

## Administrative Expenses

Salaries, wages, benefits, professional fees, vehicles and all other general and administrative expenses fall under this category. Trade license fee and other legal fees that are required to operate the retail business are also a part of administrative expenses.

## Asset

Any owned physical object (tangible) or a right (intangible) having a monetary value is called an asset. It's normally related in terms of cost (or depreciated cost).

## Balance Sheet

The portion of the financial statement that shows the financial health of a business during a selected period is called a balance sheet. It shows assets, liabilities, and shareholder's equity, and always balances according to the formula *Assets = Liabilities + Equity*.

## Beginning Inventory

It is usually expressed as the actual cost of the total inventory in hand at the beginning of an accounting period. It is the same number as the ending inventory for the previous period.

## Cash Flow

The most important way to manage a small business, cash flow reflects the flow of funds into and out of a business. The better your cash flow, the better you are able to pay expenses and pay down debt

## Cash Flow Budget

It is a projection of cash receipts and cash expenses for a period of time into the future, usually done on a monthly basis.

## Cost of Goods Sold

The cost of your inventory (goods) calculated by adding the opening inventory to the purchases at cost, minus the closing inventory at cost. This calculation may include markdowns or freight.

## Current Assets

Current assets are the assets which are expected to convert to cash usually within one year. Includes cash on hand, accounts receivable, and current inventory.

## Current Liabilities

Current liabilities are the ones which are due to be paid within one operating cycle (usually one year). It includes accounts payable, notes or bank loans payable, accrued expenses and current portion of long-term debt.

## Depreciation

Depreciation is the decline in value of a fixed asset due to wear and tear and/or obsolescence. For example, the value of your POS system in your store will decline as it ages. By depreciating the asset, you are maintaining a more accurate view of the asset on your books.

## Equity

Equity is a balance sheet category listing the shareholder's share of the company; also referred to as "net worth". It is calculated as total assets minus total liabilities.

## Financial Statement

The balance sheet and the profit and loss statement are generally spoken of as the financial statement. These reports reflect both the current financial status at the end of the accounting period and the change in financial status during the accounting period.

## Fixed Assets

These are the assets that are not brought to be sold or easily converted to cash within one year. Examples of these items would include signage, furniture, fixtures, POS equipment, leasehold improvements, or delivery vehicles.

G.M.R.O.I. - Gross Margin Return on Inventory Investment

This calculation measures your inventory's effectiveness by comparing the returns in gross margin dollars for each dollar spent in inventory.

**GMROI** (**G**ross **M**argin **R**eturn **O**n **I**nvestment) = (GM% x turnover) / (1 - markup %)

Let's understand it by using an example of how to calculate one's return on investment, **(ROI)**.

Last month, the stores sales were $ 220,000, beginning inventory was $400,000, and ending inventory was $440,000. During the month, business maintained a mark-up of 28%.

The formula for reaching the ROI in this scenario would be as follows.

Last month sales $220,000 x 28% (markup) = $61,600

Beginning Inventory$400,000+Ending Inventory $440,000 = $840,000 divided by 2 = $420,000

## Now divide

$61,600 divided by $420,000 = 14.6 % ROI (Return on Investment)

## Net Operating Income

It is the net sales minus net cost of goods sold minus operating expenses. Though often confused, this is not the same as net profit (see below formula for net profit).

## Net Profit

Normally the last line on an income statement (P&L) shows gross profit from sales minus *all* expenses (operating expenses, taxes, depreciation and withdrawals.)

## Net Worth

It is the difference between the total value of the assets minus the liabilities.

## Return on Total Assets

It is calculated as the net profit before taxes / total assets. It measures profit as a percentage of total assets.

## Selling Expenses

It's a calculation relating the expenses related to selling your merchandise and not the COGS themselves. It includes compensation (salaries, bonuses or commissions), related payroll taxes and employee benefits. It should also include advertising and marketing expenses.

## Shrinkage

It is the difference between the amount of inventory shown on the books and the actual physical inventory when counted. This will also reflect the theft. It is best to compare it to other stores in the same category. It should be the lower the better.

## Working Capital

The amount of money which may be available in order to meet current debt obligations when they become due is called working capital. This is calculated by taking your current assets and subtracting your current liabilities.

## Basics of Retailing

Now geared with important formulae and terms, you need to know the most important factor that can make or break your retail business - the Location.

I shall provide 6 secret techniques, which are my learnings for the past two decades in retail and shall make you successful in your retail career.

## 1. Pre-checklist for retailers

a) Define & classify your product type

Are you selling specialty goods, convenience goods, fashion, high ticket items etc.? Your answers will define your location requirements.

b) Determine how much retail space, storage area, or the size of the shop you will need.

## 2. Demographics & Area profiling check

Use the economic data to find out the population living in your proposed retail location catchment area. Are they your target customers? What is their household income?

Another way to look at this is from your customer's point of view.

Where would your customer prefer you to be located?

If you're a doctor or a lawyer, would the customers prefer a central location- near a hospital or the court house?

If you own a coffee shop, wouldn't you attract office goers if you opt for a location in office districts?

Put yourself in your buyer's shoes.

## 3. Accessibility, Visibility & Footfall

Look for a location that's easy to see and find, with plenty of customer parking in the front. Consider convenience of vendors in delivering inventory. For example, if you're opening a family entertainment concept, you need enough space for your amusement rides and the area should be accessible to family hangouts like food courts etc.

Visibility is of core essence. A good retail location is worth millions of online impressions or front page insertions in popular newspapers. Analyze the visibility from the number of people who pass through it, seeing your visible signage and branding.

Concepts like ultra-niche luxury, high ticket items prefer to have their own zoning inside the mall to maintain privacy and high brand imagery as they want only potential customers to visit their zone.

### 4. Brand adjacencies – Make or break factor

It is important for brands to know with whom they are hanging around. Are their neighboring brands complimenting or competing businesses?

If you want to sell high-end women's apparel, locating near other upscale women's apparel, make-up salon or a jewelry stores is a plus, because apparel shoppers visit several stores and these stores attracts a similar target audience i.e. fashion conscious customers.

But, an office supplies store wouldn't want a similar store down the street. Locations near restaurants or entertainment venues, or even a big-box store, can benefit your store if those businesses attract your target customer base.

### 5. Understand your lease offerings before signing

Check the deliverables offered in your lease agreement. Check the number. of parking lots allocated to your brand (in case you are an anchor tenant and need dedicated parking spaces). Check on the facilities and common area charges that have quoted in your lease agreement. These are the main factors which inflate your rentals. Look out for marketing fees; higher fees would make your P&L unfeasible.

But if you're looking to launch a new business in a retail space, don't let the lure of low rent tempt you into a lease deal. This can kill your business before it ever gets off the ground. And don't let a higher lease or rent payment scare you. If a location offers prime foot-traffic, walk-ins and easy access for your customers, it may be well worth the investment. In this context, your lease is simply part of your marketing spending to get people inside your store.

### 6. Compliance with local laws and authorities

Follow the local regulations and restrictions, check out the employee's recruitment criteria's, there are certain regulations stating employment for certain nationalities/ locals etc. Check out the working hours for the shopping centers since longer duration means more manpower for your shop operations which might hamper your store P&L.

In subsequent chapters, you shall learn about the future of retail and how important it is to understand your customer, their buying habits and behaviors and how you can influence those to benefit your retail business.

# Chapter 2

## What future holds for retail?

The Future of Retail is very bright.

We all hear or read about shops closures and big retail chains going bankrupt etc. but let me reiterate that there are brands like nasty gal (fast fashion), dollar shave club etc. who did not exist 10 years back and have arisen in current scenario; Thanks to digitization of retail and Omni channel retailing.

One of the trends which is being observed is

***Reverse traffic from Online to Physical stores***

According to Google, 75% of the shoppers are more likely to visit Brick & mortar stores if they find helpful local retail information in online search results.

In fact, some of the biggest players in the industry are spending billions of dollars to remodel their existing shops, hoping to lure customers inside with more modern fixtures, easier checkout options, and online order pickup kiosks.

Today, If you ask any big brick & mortar Retailer as to who is their biggest competitor, the answer would be undoubtedly "Amazon.com".

The real fact is actually that, Amazon.com is itself investing heavily in its own real estate and opening stores ranging from its cashier-less "Go" convenience shops, novelty "4 Star" locations to bookstores.

It's also shaking up the grocery industry with its acquisition of Whole Foods, pushing companies like Kroger to think outside the box.

Those of you don't know about retail brand Kroger then let me enlighten you by saying that Kroger is the biggest supermarket chain by revenue in the United States of America.

## Future is Retail 3.0

I would relate this concept of Retail 3.0 to Indian Holy Scripture "Bhagavad Gita" which professes the concept of "Vasudeva kutumbh" which means nothing but Globalization (world is your market place)

In Bhagavad Gita there is a word called "tathastu" which means literally " You ask & You get it" & that's what is the main premise of Retail 3.0 i.e. how to make the lives of shoppers more convenient by using technology as main ingredient.

## What is Retail 3.0?

Retail 3.0 is the evolution of multi-channel retail distribution. It blends technology with physical brick & mortar retail.

It makes customers (millennials) experience the brand and store more holistically by engaging them & reducing their pain points which a conventional shopping brings with it, for example carrying loads of shopping bags post shopping to your vehicle and back home.

It provides convenience and increases the brand recall as the shopper has got himself or herself personally involved in shopping experience both at emotional and intellectual levels. Hence he/she can turn out to be brand's influencers thus generating more feet-ins and brand recall through social media.

## How brands have adapted Retail 3.0?

### Case 1

**Company: Bonobos** – It is a men's clothing store wherein a shopper goes and tries out clothes. If the shopper likes it, he buy it online and the garment gets delivered to their home.

**Customer Benefit:** No hassles of carrying shopping bags.

**Retailer's benefit :** Their Retail concept requires smaller area stores that carries limited inventory as it does not require stock room resulting in addition of more trial rooms for the customers to try merchandise. Smaller spaces mean lower rentals and lower inventory holding costs and thus more operational efficiencies.

### Case 2

**Hointer**5 : It is a store wherein you can scan the type of denim jeans and the brand of jeans that you want using an app and that very pair of jeans that you want to try on will be delivered to a specific dressing room within the selected store of your choice.

Upon trying you may buy it from an app or in case you decide not to purchase, you drop the garment to an allocated shelf and the garment is removed from the app automatically as well.

### Case 3

### The Store

This brand based in Berlin is a unique example of Retail 3.0. Brand is basically a fashion brand but the owners decided to do things differently and stand out from the clutter of fashion brands. They inserted a co-working space, restaurant, hair salon and music pods. They have created a space where their customers could spend whole day lounging within the store.

**Result**: Increased dwelling times, Increase in ATV, Increase in feet-ins, higher stock-turns of merchandise, regular visits from fashionistas resulting in free word of mouth advertising as fashion influencers were clicking pictures of new merchandise and posting it on their social networks while enjoying free instore wi-fi and sipping their favorite blend of coffee.

# Chapter 3

## Understanding your customers- prime importance

4 P's of marketing which are the founding principles of marketing (Kotler's) have transformed now and evolved to 4 A's.

### Acceptability

- Accessibility
- Affordability
- Availability

I feel, since the terminology has changed, the basic principles still remain valid. One of the important points that come under Acceptability is **Consumer behavior.**

Even before SMEs or entrepreneur ventures are out to launch or introduce a service they need to ensure

- Whether there exists a market for their product or services?
- What does their targeted customers or audience perceive about their product and services?
- Analyze what pain points are your business trying to solve.

- Will consumers pay your business venture for the services in lieu of alleviating their pain points?
- Reconfirm if the customers really consider those factors or services as solutions for their problems.

Entrepreneurs often forget the importance of consumer behavior and get engrossed in other 4 P's of marketing.

It is the customer who is the core of organization and all tasks (activities or product or services) should either make difference in his life by making his life easier.

We call this approach as customer centric approach. Evaluate your promotional ideas or campaigns, if they are adding value to your customer, or they are just another piece of boring advertising.

Consumer behavior decision examines the "processes, especially any particular trigger that compels consumers to buy a certain product." This is vital for entrepreneurial ventures.

## Case study: Gillette launch in India

When international giant brand Gillette entered the Indian market, way back in 1984, they brought their best seller from the US market which was primarily a twin blade razor with a plastic tab on top, which enables easy removal of hair which used to get stuck between twin blades. They did comprehensive research on this product in MIT University, USA amongst a group of Indian students who were studying there.

The outcome was that the Gillette's twin blade product in India bombarded. They recognized that their best product failed to compel & satisfy Indian users. People who bought the razors were not satisfied with the shaving outcome.

Gillette team analyzed the core behavior of their customers and found that their best razor had failed to deliver to

Indian customer's satisfaction due to the following reasons:-

- Indians tend to have rough or hard skin and hence the beard hair needed more precision shaving products.
- India as a country always had issues with running tap water, majority of the people used stored water in a bowl (popularly known as mug) for carrying out their shaving regime, due to this their key USP of plastic tab between the blades had failed since it required running tap water.
- Indian water is hard water compared to the western countries wherein the water is soft, which failed to deliver a good shaving experience.

Once Gillette understood this consumer segment, the company created a new customized product. Gillette Guard, the first product created just for the Indian market, was introduced in October 2010. It was priced at just Rs15 per razor - less than 35 cents and three per cent of the top-of the-range Fusion Pro Glide price. At Rs 5 for a refill cartridge, Gillette Guard met customer expectations on safety and ease of use.

In Business terminology we call this as "reverse innovation" i.e. to develop a product that would satisfy the needs of the lower income customer.

They tweaked their communication with some more aspirations around the brand by asking the targeted customers; Are clean-shaven men more successful? Did the nation prefer clean-shaven celebrities? And the biggest one: do women prefer clean-shaven men? The media picked up the campaign and the brand got significant reach in minimal time span. Today, Gillette India is one of the category leaders in shaving products sector.

## Learning's for start-ups

Above case study explains the importance of reverse Innovation.

In today's technological advance systems, it's easy to create a product or a service but it is very difficult to find a customer who would pay for your product or services. Hence understanding consumer behavior is of utmost importance even before venturing out with any kind of start-ups.

Today's customers expect customization and speed of delivery in whatever they may choose to buy. Customization or personalization is also a tool used by retailers to build relationship bond with their customers.

**Case study–** Nike store, Soho, New York, USA

As you enter Soho's Nike store, you shall find in the middle of the ground floor, a shoe customization section. A customer can choose one of Nike's latest model shoes, such as the Nike Air, choose any of the five colors, and watch their custom shoe get created, along with a crowd taking photos and posting them.

Nike has invented a process to create truly unique shoes, simplifying the process by starting with one color— white— creating a pair of custom shoes in minutes, and getting free promotion from other consumers posting and sharing images.

While Nike has been customizing shoes online for some time, seeing and experiencing the process and customer reactions in store is completely a mesmerizing experience.

Nike has harnessed its capabilities to deal with the competing forces of customization, speed, and scale; plus, it's using the in-store experience to demonstrate how innovative the brand really is.

The store narrates the concept of personalizing their shoe as a story & the result is that the store gets packed with locals and tourists, and the creation of every shoe becomes an event. People get captivated by the cool technology, and they share the experience instantly through photos and videos.

Thus Nike is a great experience creator and story teller.

# Chapter 4

## What factors can make or break your retail brand?

I have always noticed that most of the Retail CEOs/ CFOs often take a downward look when it comes to "Markdowns".

I recall, my previous boss (who is also my mentor) who used to give me a very awkward and nasty look every time I proposed using Markdowns as Marketing tool/ event.

This chapter will talk about how markdown planning can help retailers increase sales & improve margins. We shall talk about "open to Buy" as strategic planning tool and we shall also learn about as to avoid stock loss i.e. Retail Shrinkage in retail store.

This chapter is my attempt to clear some concepts and convince senior management to adapt to this wonderful planning tool which can prove to be very effective in their Inventory Planning goals.

Markdowns are often associated with margin degradation and profit loss— and some companies believe that cutting prices for their products could negatively impact their brand image. Although inevitable, retailers have historically viewed markdowns as a necessary evil designed to help sell old or slow-moving inventory.

(A) View Markdowns as a function of Price Elasticity: matching perceptions with pricing.

An example of a markdown would be if you had a sweat shirt for sale that was originally priced at Dhs100 and after one month of slow sales, you decide to markdown the sweatshirt at 20% off, making it Dhs80 at retail.

Although you just lost Dhs20 of your intended markup on that sweat shirt, but in return, you are also inviting more people to purchase it at a price they may prefer vis a vis the original Dhs 100 price. Since, the sweat shirt had not been selling well at Dhs100, offering a nice, mark-downed price can often result in sales that would not happen otherwise. Hopefully a 20% discount will do the trick, however often you will find that you need to continue your markdown strategies based on slow sales, moving the product from 20% off to 30%, 40% and more if necessary.

Most retail CEOs and CFOs (especially organizations run by finance professionals and not by Retail mindset professionals) often confuse markdowns with discounts model.

A discount is a reduction in the price of an item or transaction based upon the customer making the purchase. Many retailers offer discounts because they find that customers return to their store versus others because of the discount provided to them. Discount offers "Instant gratification".

Customers often enjoy the advantages they feel that discounts give, such as being a preferred customer and therefore getting special treatment. Some boutiques & spas offer friends and families discounts, which benefits both the retailer and those getting the discounts. It's a win-win on both sides.

Both a markdown and a discount can be temporary or permanent, depending on how you market them to your customers.

An example of a temporary discount would be to get a discount equivalent to your waist size. If your waist size is 34 then avail 34% discount on your purchases.

A temporary markdown example would be if you had a one day sale, offering marked down prices for only a specific amount of time.

Discount strategy is more tactical whereas markdown strategy is more organic in nature. Both should be an integral part of marketing mix.

I recall a statement of Sir Martin Sorrell (CEO, WPP- an advertising agencies conglomerate), who once quipped, "Discounts are like bad cholesterol and markdowns are like good cholesterol; there has to be less dependence on discounting model, instead push more brand-building efforts".

(B) Using markdowns to control Inventory Ageing

You can use both discounts and markdowns as a part of your sales strategy to help make the most out of your inventory sell through and ultimately, your sales goals.

Wasting your retail floor space with products that are not selling will not help you at all, so consider how markdowns and discounts may be able to work for you in your sales strategy.

(C) Tie your Markdown planning with your financial plan- how much hit are you willing to take in markdowns?

A markdown plan means nothing if it's not tied into the financial plan. Retailers should determine how much they are willing to spend on markdowns to hit their financial targets. This information ideally flows either from CFO/ CEOs while preparing budgets for next fiscal.

It's equally as important that retailers are able to not only execute on the markdown plan once it's in place, but also monitor it in real time. This will ensure that adjustments can be made as the season progresses.

D) Determine early the items that you are willing to reduce the price over time and how much

It implies whether you want to run it on category or on specific collections. Monitor its sales through rate and then decide the markdown %.

(E) Managing Product life-cycles more effectively

Smart retailers will leverage effective markdown planning to not only ensure that there is less stock left over at the end of the season, but to also manage new product introductions and phase-outs.

Caution to retailers who shy away from markdowns strategy Retailers that avoid putting a markdown plan in place may experience increased cannibalization of new product lines and decreased sales.

The impact could even extend to the store level as new and old products are shoved together on store shelves or displays, resulting in cluttered and disorganized stores that even the most loyal customers will find difficult to shop in.

A perfect example is "Part Sale" that we find very commonly in retail stores these days in the Middle East, wherein new merchandise is being sold with that of discounted merchandise in a separate enclosures or gondolas.

## What is OTB?

An Open-To-Buy is a budget that involves the full range of budgetary functions. It begins with the planning process, is future oriented, provides guidance on how much to buy, and provides benchmarks for evaluating progress, and adjusting future plans.

Having too much inventory (or the wrong type) during certain periods can slow your cash flow and reduce profits with too many markdowns. On the other hand, if you under-buy (meaning buy too little product) and miss sales opportunities, then you are not making your potential profit (plus damaging the customer experience). A retailer can be sure to stock the right amount of the right products at the right time by using an Open-to-Buy plan.

## How to calculate OTB – its formula?

As per retail textbook, its formula is simple i.e.

EOM (end of month stock level-desired estimate)

+ Sales (month actual)

+ Markdowns (month actual)

– BOM (beginning of month stock level-actual)

– Merchandise on order (or stock in pipeline/transit).

---

= Open-to-Buy (Dhs/ AED amount available for new purchases)

For example, a retailer has an inventory level of Dhs 150,000 on March 1st and planned Dhs 152,000/- End of Month inventory for March 31st. The planned sales for the store are Dhs 78,000 with Dhs 7500 in planned markdowns. Therefore, the retailer has Dhs 87,500/- Open-To-Buy at retail. (Here there is no merchandise on order).

Now if you operate your brand at 50% margins then multiply Dhs 87500 x 50% , you shall get OTB budget at cost i.e. Dhs 43,750/-

In other words, it describes how much inventory can I buy without getting myself in trouble? It is also the process of planning merchandise sales and purchases.

## Advantages

OTB brings a balance to stock at hand inventory and future purchasing. This balance allows you to respond to selling trends in a timely fashion.

Since I have been personally involved in leasing management i.e. location scouting for brands that I have handled in the past and currently, I shall explain this in easier layman terms.

Consider that the merchandise sitting on that shelf is the tenant. Good tenants pay the rent on time by 'turning' or selling frequently. Bad tenants are the ones that don't sell quickly and sit on the shelf for months. They take up valuable selling space that could and should be given to a faster moving product.

As a landlord, ask yourself how long can you afford to have non-paying tenants on your shelves before it negatively effects the total retail operation?

Good inventory control is critical to ensuring an adequate level of stock is at hand for the number of sales being generated.

My personal advice (based on my retail experience in Material resource planning with leading Middle Eastern retailer) is as under

a) Before placing your Open-to-Buy plan into operation, ask yourself if each number is realistic. Does it make sense for the way you do business? Keep in mind that many of the figures in your inventory plan are only guidelines. A good rule of thumb is if your actual ending inventory is within

6-8 percent of your plan, then you are doing very well.

b) Be cautious about offers of quantity discounts or free freight if you increase the size of your order significantly over your normal purchasing levels. Most suppliers tend to offer free freight if brands commit to buy certain quantities and this is a trap as the supplier is trying to upsell his quantities to you with an incentive.

c) Don't hesitate to markdown slow moving merchandise. Make the markdown instantly appealing to the customer by offering at least 25% to 40% off the retail price. The faster it is off your shelves, the faster you can bring in a better-selling product that will have a higher profit margin

In the case of fashion or seasonal merchandise, an Open-To-Buy answers the question of how much to buy, but not necessarily the question of which specific items to buy. For that, a detailed assortment plan is necessary.

## How the planning process works?

The planning process begins with building a sales plan.

Once a sales plan has been developed, the next piece of the planning process is to build an inventory plan. The question to ask is this- "How much inventory do I need at the end of each month to support the next month's sales (in some cases the ending inventory may need to support more than just one month of future sales), as well as maintain effective merchandise displays?"

From there, other things like inventory adjustments and markdowns need to be planned.

Finally, from the plans that have been developed, an inventory receipt plan can be arrived at. For any given period (month or week), the planned inventory receipts is the planned ending inventory, plus the planned sales, markdowns and inventory adjustments, less the prior month's ending inventory. Stated another way, the planned inventory receipts answers the question, "How much inventory do I need to bring in to cover my sales, markdowns and adjustments, given my planned beginning inventory, in order to end up with my planned ending inventory?"

## Case study

Brand Benetton uses this statistical tool very innovatively along with their supply chain strategy.

Normally brands in traditional/conventional way of production, dyes complete cotton yarn with specific colors and then produce garments like sweat shirts, tees etc. but Benetton does it differently.

Benetton dyes only certain quantities of sweat shirts, tees etc. in various colors and sends to its stores Then based on the sales movement of specific color and type (tees, sweat shirts) they dye the complete yarn with color that is fast moving in their stores.

My friends in retail would argue about the loss of time in getting the feedback from stores about which color is moving fast, that's where your smart MIS systems comes to play, which can give you reports in a dashboard format.

Benetton has mastered this function of getting the feedback from the shop floor to production lines in minimal time period and thus they avoid producing colors that would not sell or move thus preventing overstock at production facility stage itself.

This is what I call learning from internal systems and continuously improving your processes to optimize returns or retail dollars.

## What Is Retail Shrinkage?

Retail shrinkage is the portion of your inventory that gets lost or stolen. It is expressed as a percentage i.e. value of lost or stolen stock divided by overall sales.

## Why retail shrinkage causes headache to retailers?

As if the shift to online shopping wasn't enough of a headache for cash-strapped retailers, they're also increasingly worried about "shrinkage."

"Retail Shrinkage" of 4% can wipe off 12% of your Net profit, leaving the cash strapped retailer in a chaos, thinking what has hit them unknowingly.

A survey done in United States by the National Retail Federation found annually there is a loss of approx. $48 billion to retailers through shrinkage.

## How to prevent retail shrinkage in Retail?

With the advent of technology, this task has become less painful but I strongly believe in following the basic principles of Loss Prevention methodology in order to achieve your organization's goal.

1. Commitment from Top management and Brand owners
2. Any strategic change can only be implemented successfully if there is a complete 100% commitment from the top management or brand owners.
3. Build strong Internal audit function

   Develop an Environment of Loss Prevention in overall organization by:

- By making employees accountable: Employees throughout the company must take responsibility for reducing shrinkage. The company should see loss prevention as equal to sales in importance.
- Train staff to follow Security Policies and Procedures: Not only retail sales staff needs to be trained but also warehousing staff who are responsible for processing sales request or sales order i.e. reduce variances or shrinkage by correctly picking and packing an item for the store and by proper documentation data entry at the time of processing delivery notes.

4. Customer Service

   One of the best deterrents against shoplifting is good customer service. The elements of friendly, helpful service naturally conflict with the accessible environment shoplifters want.

   Greeting customers when they come in the store makes them aware that you notice their presence. Approaching them to ask if they need help and checking in periodically helps prevent them from feeling comfortable enough to steal.

5. Consider Your Store Layout

   An open floor plan where retail sales staff or service associates can see much of the store from central locations helps as well.

6. Technology

   Technology also is used to deter stealing. Security cameras and electronic surveillance tags and scanners are among the more common tools used to prevent shoplifting. Electronic tags and scanners are used to signal loss prevention employees when someone tries to slip out the door without paying for an item and having the tag removed.

7. Preventing Non-Shoplifting Shrinkage

   Minimizing or eliminating employee theft is a challenge. Building a trusting environment with a motivated work force is the ideal starting point. If employees are motivated, fairly paid and empowered, they are less likely to feel compelled to steal.

It should be a common goal for all retail floor staff to prevent accounting errors and fraud. Employees need to accurately count products when they arrive and compare them against Delivery note or what the Point of sales system says they should receive.

8. Annual or Bi-annual Stock audit

   Count the physical inventory in your business every year or twice a year to take corrective steps.

## Case study:

A recent study done by an auditing firm on Loss prevention program by studying companies like Target, Limited Brands, Best Buy, Gap, and CVS.

Their findings were eye-opener, the average shrinkage rate of these five companies was 44% below the U.S. mean, and one company's rate was 70% below.

Some unique processes that these companies followed that made them stand apart (including points mentioned above) are-

## Using evidence-based management

Decisions must be derived from detailed and timely data, not intuition. (Most of the five companies' store managers received item-level shrinkage data every week.)

## Linking shrinkage to KPIs

Companies can help keep shrinkage on the agenda by, for example, providing regular shrinkage scorecards, linking it individual staffs KPI's and using it at the time of appraisals.

These companies have shown that demonstrating strong leadership, embedding effective procedures, and ensuring compliance can drastically limit situations where shrinkage can occur.

# Chapter 5

## Logistics- its role in retail

Ever wondered how the goods arrive at store shelves and then later to customer's homes (in case of ecommerce), it is all because of supply chain or in ecommerce retail it's called Last mile Logistics.

All the processes that you utilize to ensure your products reach the customers, starting from obtaining the raw materials, managing inbound materials & production processes to last-mile delivery of those products at your customer's doorstep, are together known as retail supply chain.

When you optimize all these processes to increase both speed and efficiency, it becomes retail supply chain management.

Brands like Zara and H&M are called as genius due to logistics as they mastered the art of supply chain to their advantage i.e. by identifying the right trends, producing the garment at their 3rd party sites across the globe (Zara utilized the local Spanish cottage industries as their core suppliers initially) and then shipping the items to their warehouses in minimal time required. The success of retail brand depends upon their supply chains and how efficiently they can manage it.

The importance of logistics is far beyond the scope of this chapter hence I shall touch up Last Mile logistics as it is the most crucial aspect for Omni channel retailing.

## What is "Last mile logistics"?

Last mile logistics refers to the final step of the delivery process from a distribution center or facility to the end user. Although the name implies, it is the final mile delivery, actual last mile delivery can range from a few blocks to 50 or 100 miles.

Most often, last mile logistics involves the use of courier or small package carriers to deliver products to consumers.

## Why is it crucial for e-tailers or e-commerce players?

It's pertinent to understand the logistics process in any e-commerce company.

The Logistics Cycle in e-commerce can be broken down into 5 major components, first-mile delivery, fulfillment, processing/sorting, line haul and last-mile delivery. (For some lean start-ups, it involves 3-4 components only)

## First-mile delivery

This involves picking up goods from the sellers and transporting it to the e-commerce retailer's fulfillment center or directly to the mother warehouse.

## Fulfillment

Post first mile logistics, the next phase that follows is fulfillment, which involves picking and packaging of products once an order is placed on the website and then moving it to the mother warehouse.

## Sorting

After fulfillment, the products are sorted on the basis of the final delivery location.

## Line-haul

This stage involves connecting the main supply center with the main demand center, via land or air.

## Last-mile delivery

This is the last however the most important phase of the logistics cycle involving the dispatch and shipping of products from the mother hubs and to the delivery hubs, from where they are delivered to the end-customers.

The reason why "Last-mile delivery" becomes critical is due to the fact that majority of customer complaints in any e-commerce company are **pertaining "Late deliveries"** which are mainly due to lack of processes in workforce management, no real time coordination between fulfillment teams and last mile delivery teams.

**Customer returns** and the ability of a retailer to quickly process the returns to enrich customer experience is another major challenge faced by e-commerce retailers.

## The emergence of new entrants in "Last mile logistics"

Companies such as Amazon have already jumped into the fray with its Amazon Prime Air service that it hopes will soon use small drones to deliver packages in 30 minutes or less. Drones, droids, and parcel copters are here to stay.

## Future for Last mile logistics companies

Companies like Uber eats, Deliveroo has mastered the model of Airbnb but for transportation/logistics.

Technology has allowed these companies to leverage their advantage and offer jobs to anyone with a car or bike. They are able to analyze data and figure out how to do the job for less. They can fill capacity in vehicles that weren't previously open to them.

I feel the future for Last mile logistics providers is very promising provided they adapt to technology advancements at the earliest & ride the disruption wave.

**Case study:** Carrefour Valet trolley (home delivery services) available in Dubai

Hypermarket giants like Carrefour have been fast enough to realize the importance & advantages of last-mile logistics for enhancing their customer experience and also leading to customer retention strategy.

Today in Dubai, Carrefour offers Valet trolley facility to its customers. Leave your trolley at their store and have your items delivered to your doorstep at your convenience.

## The benefit to customers

Convenient shopping experience without going through hassles of pulling overloaded trolleys to parking lots etc.

# Chapter 6

## How to Franchise your business?

As this is one topic that I am very passionate about and had a privilege of working under both franchisor and franchisee in the past. I would dedicate this chapter to my mentors/ bosses who gave me the opportunity to learn about franchising in a more practical way rather than a theoretical manner.

### What is franchising?

Franchising is a business relationship in which the franchisor (the owner of the business providing the product or service) assigns to independent people (the franchisees) the right to market and distribute the franchisor's goods or service and to use the business' name for a fixed period of time.

*"Franchising works by combining the drive and energy of the entrepreneur with the experience and expertise of the franchisor."*

### Benefits of franchising for entrepreneurs

- Be your own boss
- Tested business model
- Training & Marketing support

- Support in site/location selection
- Networking with peers/partners in other territories to learn from their experiences.
- The cost advantage of bulk purchasing by the franchisor and the cost benefits are usually passed onto the franchisees.
- Pride of ownership of franchised brand in an exclusive territory

## So why does franchise system fail to deliver?

The main reason for the system to break down is lack of managing expectations both from franchisor's & franchisee's side. This happens when the franchisor starts seeing franchising as the fastest way to grow their riches. They are interested in signing of new franchisees and get their annual fees in return. They fail to understand that it is the successes of their franchisees that will make their mother brand succeed in new territory. *"Take care of your franchisees and they shall in return take care of your business and your brand in their territories"* is one of the mantras for the success of the franchise system.

## Few questions that need to be asked prior to taking any brand on franchising

1. Can you make money with this franchise? What are your COGS? What is the royalty or fees payback period? Is the franchisor ready to provide initial capex support?
2. Is the franchisor making money/ where is the money coming from? Do they have a good network of financial partners/investors/ banking institutions?
3. Does the franchisor understand franchising?

4. Are other franchisees happy with their investments?

## Word of caution for franchisees

### Do your due diligence

- Never get carried away by big promises made by franchisors, ensure that you understand all the finer details in a franchise agreement or hire a professional legal advisor to review all the agreements. Ask for franchisors income statements as you need to ensure that your franchisor's financial health is sound enough to ensure steady supply chain of goods and services to your newly formed franchised business.

- Many people mistakenly believe a franchise, although higher cost is a lower risk option – but it is not. When the franchisor is asking for 7% of turnover per month for license fees and **up to 3% of turnover per month for a marketing fund,** the franchisee has a lot of work to do before they break even. Not to mention the cost of borrowing to buy the franchise and ongoing fixed cost base.

- ***Pricing*** is a common issue in the startup of a franchise. Finding the price point between cost and profit is a must, to be successful. Every business needs to fill a gap in a market with its product or service. Hence every franchisee needs to do research as to how much his customers would be willing to pay for availing a product or service from the franchised brand. Most of the times, franchisors fail in reading this aspect of the market as they tend to evaluate multiple territories with their own base territory pricing which may or may not hold true. The best way is to use the Big Mac index while devising pricing in multiple territories.

To sum up, not all business models will be successful and nor all franchisee models would ensure your success. Hence prior to deciding to franchise your business or to purchasing an existing franchise, make sure to evaluate both pros and cons.

I have tried my best to provide an initial checklist for both franchisor and franchisee which they can follow in order to make their business successful.

## How to build a robust franchise model?

The most critical element for any franchise manager is to play a balancing act between both franchisor and franchisee. He/she has to think like an entrepreneur all the time taking care of both franchisors and franchisee's interests.

Franchising model encompasses and provides independence to the franchisee to run and operate his business but at the same time provides protocols & systems that come by having brand affiliations or along with franchise agreements.

It is the main KPI (key performance indicator) for any franchise manager to manage interests & expectations of both parties so that the model becomes profitable.

## How to play a balancing act?

Franchise managers need to spend their efforts on creating systems and process flows-

- Robust franchise agreements
- Detailed training manuals and its implementation with internal audit checks.
- Comprehensive operating manuals, guidelines, brand guidelines etc.

- Strong policies and procedures– try using automated tools here in case you have merchandise/products to handle.

From my practical experience of franchising fashion apparels and beauty brands, it is advisable to ensure that your franchise partner uses your Point Of Sales systems so that you can monitor his sales and stock levels closely and implement PUSH merchandise replenishment strategy from time to time.

It would result in faster replenishments and stock rotations thus resulting in more sales and faster break even for the franchisees.

## Types of franchise models

There are multiple ways of creating franchise models and put to test. Most common practices are-

1. Collection of franchise fees for territory allocation (master franchisee) on sign up and then X amount per location added in that territory, coupled with royalty i.e. % of sales on per annum basis.
2. Some franchisors work on X% of your gross profits.
3. Some franchisors sell their products to the franchisee on % discount and advise them on their selling retail prices thus ensuring that product sold is at uniform base pricing globally.
4. Some franchisors help franchisee build their first store by providing them with shop fittings and furniture at subsidized rates and with longer pay-back periods.

Basically, there are multiple ways you can make your franchise model customized and suited to your requirements.

Foremost point to remember, "Always think from franchisee's perspective and ask yourself, will you buy this franchise yourself with these commercials?" If the answer is yes, then you are on the right track.

Profitability varies from business to business, and industry to industry. How well a business is managed by the owner will have a significant impact on how profitable it ultimately is.

I've seen 1 million dirham businesses that don't generate any profits – or worse, are losing money.

I've also seen smaller businesses that generate only Dhs100,000 to Dhs 200,000 in gross sales, yet turn a net profit of 40 percent.

The key is to not let big top line numbers blur your judgment. The bottom line of a business is much more important.

Work out your COGS (cost of goods sold) ratio or % so that it gives enough space to your franchisee to sell and make some decent net profit post incurring all the expenses (rent, salaries, equipment, taxes, depreciation, operating costs etc.).

**Remember**:- Your franchisee's success would determine your success as a franchisor.

# Chapter 7

## Visual Merchandising- A strategic business Tool

Visual merchandising is also called "silent salesman" in retail.

During the course of my retail career, I have observed that visual merchandising which is often kept at the last number in the priority list of retail CEOs, COOs or is often left to Operations team to decide & manage along with store operation.

I feel it is important to highlight the importance of Visual Merchandising in brand building initiatives and developing loyal customers for the brand.

During the course of my retail journey, I got hands-on experience in managing VM teams and leading VM functions for couple of middle-eastern brands in my retail career and I have often considered it and have given this function more priority than marketing or advertising functions in retail mix.

It is my sincere attempt to clarify some fundamental principles of Visual Merchandising to brand owners, retailers and retail professionals so that they can re-energize their brands using Visual Merchandising strategy.

## What is Visual Merchandising?

Visual Merchandising, also known as the 'silent salesman', suggests selling by display and presentation. Its focal points are situated strategically to circulate the customer in the store and communicate the capabilities and advantages of the merchandise.

This is completed by converting a passerby to a browser with a successful window display, a browser to a spender via the process of 'conversion', a spender to a major spender by increasing the 'ticket size' assisted by the method of cross-merchandising.

## Extension of brand's identity and communication

Visual merchandising is an extension of brand's image and should be in sync with brand's communication strategy.

## Imparting outstanding Shopping Experience

Visual merchandising enhances the shopping experience by creating suitable ambience, producing an image of the store in the minds of the customers via a combination of colors, display presentations, graphics, lighting, forms and fixtures. If completed in an exciting and dynamic fashion, the shopping experience would be pleasurable for the consumer and make him/her come repeatedly.

## Communication Tool

Visual merchandising communicates to the clients the right message about the merchandise by projecting the latest trends, colors and fashion in apparel retailing. Visual displays are great communication drivers and deliver an opportunity for retailers to sell a variety of merchandise.

## Theme displays

Based on a season or an event, a theme is employed to promote a proper product range.

## Coordinated displays

It contains items that are typically utilized/ sold/ consumed together, growing several purchases besides educating or informing the customer. Classification dominant displays contain all varieties of 1 item, are used to convey the impression of a wide selection.

## Importance of VM strategy in Purchase cycle

Consumer's perceptions, aspirations, motivations and memories play an important role in purchase cycle.

VM alters the perception and attitude of the consumers, forcing them to buy the product in a way that he/she enjoys purchasing goods thus leaving an everlasting shopping experience.

31% of the consumer's purchases in lifestyle products are impulse purchases thus a store with good displays and theme and décor attract eyeballs, thus increasing footfalls and hence converting footfall into sales.

78% of shoppers recall store name when they liked the store window display, interiors or music.

How well the store presents its merchandise using displays relates to generation of brand imagery. Involvement of sensory, emotions, attitudes during the buying process decision provides enjoyment and satisfaction to shoppers.

How Visual Merchandising helps in generating footfalls and sales?

**Exterior presentation:** sign boards, store exteriors, store signage, window displays and banners.

**Store layout:** merchandise flow, category zoning, ease in accessibility of merchandise, lighting concept.

## Store interior presentation:

merchandising principles, color coordination/ stories, merchandising techniques using mannequins, lighting, music etc., using props to highlight product, pricing signage's to communicate "Hot deals", floor and wall coverings, space design to ensure proper circulation of customers across the stores, defining hot and cold walls in store layout process.

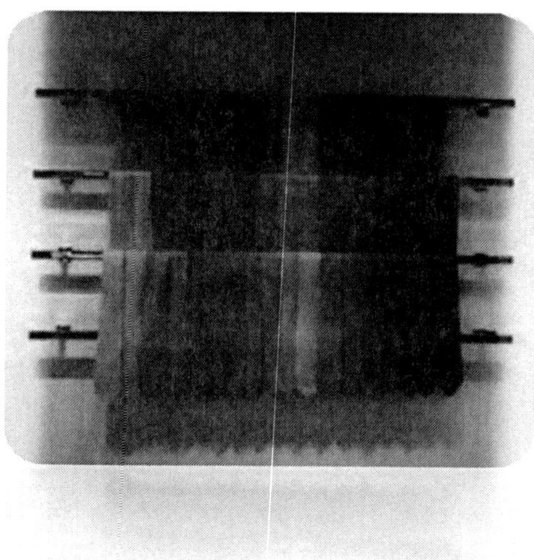

Visual Merchandising offers Multi-sensory experience for the store to its customers.

## Live Displays

These are sometimes used for product displays at the entrance of the store to demonstrate the use of products. Children's stores often use people dressed as cartoon characters to attract kids' attention.

## Island Displays

**These** are displays of merchandise found generally at the entrance of stores to announce new arrivals, special offers, etc. A display podium is erected and decorated suitably.

To sum up visual merchandising can be a key differentiator for your brand. It is a form of storytelling by wrapping your merchandise in to stories and engaging customers through visually engaging and enticing props.

# Chapter 8

## Branding In Retail Management

In this chapter let's discuss about how you can build your retail brand using social media, strategies that you need to incorporate and learn how brands are thriving even in era of economic slowdown.

The most common mindset in today's retail companies pertaining social media is that they feel that by assigning one additional social media expert resource (head count) to their existing marketing team would get them to top of the mind recall in their targeted customer's minds.

Few premises for the above belief in many retail companies

a) Social media is easy to handle and does not require great efforts or any specialized skill-set resource.

b) Posting about their services and offers is all they mean with "content". Flashy artworks, offers/promotions and beautiful product shots are all they know about content management.

c) They fail to identify, social media channels as a source of revenue and customer engagement.

With the popularity of Instagram Stories, Facebook Live, and messenger apps have fundamentally changed how retailers interact with consumers online.

Simply posting photos or updates to a branded social profile won't cut it anymore.

Need some food for thought for reconsidering your social media strategies? Here are a few retailers that have winning social media strategies:

## Case 1: Birchbox

Birchbox uses Facebook Live to share great content and engage with fans. The cosmetic brand regularly runs Facebook Live videos in which members of the company share news, give away prizes, and answer questions on the air.

According to Marketing Dive, Birchbox's top performing stream "lasted 40 minutes and had an average view time of 10 minutes among the nearly 50,000 viewers who participated live."

## Strategy delivering result:-

Birchbox sees live video as a two-way street. Not only does the Birchbox engage with target audiences in real-time, but it also allows consumers to interact with the brand. The retailer approaches live stream as Q&A opportunities with audiences where Birchbox can market the products included in their monthly subscription boxes and educate audiences about the brand.

While some Middle Eastern retailers might still be wondering whether to consider live video as part of their strategies, Birchbox (the online beauty retailer) has been bullish from the start and is an early adopter of Facebook's new live video feature.

## Key point takeaways:-

The primary function of any advertising is to influence and trigger "call to action" amongst its consumers to buy something.

## Advertising is an art of persuasion:-

Understanding how persuasion techniques are used in advertising is a science to reckon.

Persuasion techniques can be rational, irrational or emotional or combination of all three. You need to incorporate the same in your social media communication strategy.

## How to survive in an era of digital disruptions?

We live in an environment wherein everything can be copied;, any innovation can be copied and launched in a better and fine-tuned service or in form of a product.

No copyright law suit or trademark can protect your innovation or innovative service. There is always a way out in legal terminology which we call as loopholes.

In this chapter we shall discover some case studies, some tricks & strategies for the businesses to overcome this problem and would help you become a disruptor in your own domain or category of expertise.

**Rule no 1**- If you cannot beat the opponent, change the rules of the game.

**Case study:** Harry's a hip & trendy razor club.

Razor category is dominated by P&G Gillette and the founders of Harry's were quick to realize that they cannot afford to fight with the MNC giant.

Using digital platform and using influencer based content;, Harry's launched their trendy razor subscription service.

Today, Harry's, attracts more Instagram followers and product subscriptions through its website than a fully stocked Gillette aisle in a supermarket ever could. And so, Harry's has been growing 35% year-on-year between 2014 to 2016, which is three times faster than the industry average, commanding 9% of all online razor sales.

Whereas the Gillette aisle in the local supermarket targets exactly one catchment area or the neighborhood, Harry's website reaches millions.

Yes, the market share of Harry's is fractional when compared to Gillette but it has made its presence felt in a short span of time.

**Rule no 2-** If you can't reinvent yourself then buy out your competition

Unilever was quick to understand the ball game of ecommerce and how it could affect their future sales especially in a category which was dominated by their rival P&G Gillette.

Unilever acquired dollar shave club for 1 billion USD. The benefits of buying out your competition are plenty- ready ecosystem of ecommerce platform, ready customer base of millions of subscribers and moreover a commanding position of a category which in this case was dominated by Gillette.

**Case study 2:** Xiaomi –Chinese mobile company.

Chinese smartphone maker, Xiaomi had invested in some 55 startups, generating products from power banks to air purifiers.

Of these companies, 29 were incubated from the ground up by Xiaomi, and four were already unicorns worth over $1 billion.

What Xiaomi offers to startups is a combination of funding and incubation by "taking non-controlling shares" and "leaving maximum interests to the startups" so that they are much more incentivized and willing to fight on the front line.

Startups typically get access to Xiaomi's brand and distribution—its online channel, its app, and its 300 offline stores. As a result, Xiaomi is poised as not only a low-cost phone maker but also an emerging powerhouse among the makers of the all-important "connected home devices."

## Advantages

Xiaomi's ecosystem gives customers unusual new products that they never knew existed.

Bluetooth speaker, internet-enabled rice cooker, and air purifier (the first affordable one in China)—products that the company claims are not only best in class but also cost less than their existing counterparts.

Xiaomi, by investing in start-ups has created an entry barrier for its competitors when it comes to innovation and developing innovative products.

That's what I call a masterstroke of a strategist.

**Rule no 3-** Leap into the future.

Take learning's from your past experiences whether good or bad and with curious minds, trying to seek new knowledge that would help you to take your business in search of new opportunities which would eventually leap forward your business.

**Rule no 4-** Execution is everything.

Everything is today's world can be copied and launched in the shortest time possible, however what cannot be copied by your competition is:

- Your passion towards your product or service
- Your hard work and persistence
- Your execution of your vision into strategy.

# Chapter 9

## Is Loyalty programs or cards still relevant?

My inspiration to write this chapter comes from the feeling that how we (marketers & retailers) tends to get myopic and lose out on overall objective or the big picture.

Securing customer's loyalty goes beyond having a loyalty programme.

Winning both Hearts and Minds are a big challenge for today's Retailers.

Explore following areas first to determine whether your company really needs loyalty programme-

a) Can you build customer's loyalty using Top of Mind recall?

b) Can you win customer's loyalty by providing him/her great in-store experience?

c) Have you evaluated the cost of acquisition of new customer vs cost of retaining existing customer? (This ratio would vary from industry to industry, for example in telecom industry (especially in Indian subcontinent) the cost of acquiring new customer is comparatively lower than retaining existing customer.)

d) Will your customer pay in advance to become a member of your loyalty club? (Read case study on this point at the end of this chapter highlighting this aspect)

If you have answered "Yes" to any above first 3 questions, then work on the same and delay launching any new loyalty programme.

The reasons for making this bold statement are as follows:

- Traditional financially driven loyalty schemes can become a financial liability for businesses if not properly planned in initial stages itself. Your initial plan should very well capture the proposed sales expected by loyalty card and expenses that would be accrued to run it smoothly.
- Traditional points-based schemes are often not agile enough to meet rapidly changing customer expectations in the same way that 'connected stores' and new technologies can engage with consumers.
- Today's customers are exposed to Giga bytes of advertising information daily that they no longer value the reward that is offered in the end (post purchase). For example, Majority of hypermarket retailers offers approx. 1% of customer's purchase as loyalty rewards i.e. On spending Dhs 2000/-, customer can expect a reward of Dhs 20/- (approx.).
- Retailers today are in kind of a rat race "Oh my competitor has loyalty programme, why should I miss the bandwagon". They tend to ignore their customer's shopping habits, their frequency of

store visits, their basket size, are they value seekers or discount lovers.

Today's retailers need to understand and accept the fact that "Loyalty" is an overused, overexploited concept and does not excite new age shoppers who are much more aware about the products & services and are more demanding. Although the word 'loyalty' is often associated with the points and financial incentive schemes that were launched over 30 years ago, these schemes have lost its relevance in current times.

**How to be a disruptor then?** (Simply by not launching a point based loyalty card/app) Loyalty should be about more than just collecting points. If not innovated, your Loyalty club would end up looking like Me-too offering.

- Segment your customers; ask your store teams as to what is making their regular customer come back to their stores.
- Use technology in making the customer's purchase cycle seamless.
- Loyalty is often tied to routine, so any innovation that simplifies a routine while enhancing the customer experience is a reward in itself.
- Understand from your customers as to what drives loyalty in them for your brand. Is it discounts, happy hours or convenience, customer service, good assortment of large merchandise offerings?

**Winning** loyalty in Digital era needs a mix of Personalization, Engagement, and a sense of Exclusivity across all different channels (instore, website, mobile app, social platforms).

As per a study done by Deloitte research when it comes to consumers attitudes to loyalty programmes, research shows that personalization and relevance are high on the list of what consumers expect from a loyalty scheme. Study showed 41percent of consumers agree with "Loyalty schemes help brands know what their customers want and provide them with helpful suggestions and rewards, (e.g. receiving vouchers and coupons on products they buy regularly)".

## Case study: Amazon Prime

Amazon Prime is an outrageously successful membership program with the stats to prove it-

- 80 million members
- $1,300 average member annual spend vs. $700 non-member
- 60% of Amazon customers are Prime Members

Amazon Prime, which offers free streaming of thousands of movies and TV shows and, most important, free two-day shipping on most Amazon purchases. The service usually costs $79 annually, though it's cheaper for college students ($39 annually, after six months free). Subscribers not only ordered more often, but after paying the $79 fee, they started buying things at Amazon that they probably wouldn't have in the past. Since shipping was always speedy and free, members saved themselves a trip to the store for things like batteries and coffee beans. Can your loyalty program boost of statistics like Amazon's Prime. If not, then your loyalty program is on its way of becoming a liability for your business. It's time to run a timely checklist and overview on your loyalty program.

I would end this chapter by a quote by Sir Terry Leahy : "The true source of loyalty is to create benefits for people."

# Chapter 10

## Entrepreneurship in Retail

Retail is one of the oldest economic activities whose evolution begins from human evolution.

With the increase in population and increase of competition across all fields, it has become difficult for a fresh graduate or a skilled graduate to get a suitable opening, hence in the current scenario, retailpreneurship offers not only job prospects but also creates an ecosystem for the new economic activity empowering our young talents to scale up their startup ideas into reality.

### It all begins with an idea...

Do you know as to how many thoughts does a human being get on an average in a day?

The answer is approx. 50,000 to 70,000 thoughts i.e. 35-50 thoughts per minute. Some thoughts are negative in nature and few positive ones convert into ideas.

The complexity grows when you are running or about to begin your startup company. Foremost thing that you need in any business or profession is FOCUS.

We need to train or code our mind to say NO to many thoughts/ Ideas in order to keep progressing on one particular idea or goal and remain focused on your goal.

We get ideas for new features to be added to our product or new product development, on top of it, we also get dozens of good ideas from our customers too. But if we keep chasing these wonderful ideas, we shall not reach anywhere. (It's like a treadmill wherein you never get anywhere.).

## So what do business owners do in such cases?

Firstly, don't get excited in the heat of the moment with great ideas, instead, write it down and park it for a couple of weeks and revisit them with a calm mind and see if it really makes sense to add this idea in your current product in order to add value to its customers. How much additional resource would new ideas take in order to execute? Analyze the cost-benefit aspect and then decide.

Secondly, you as an entrepreneur or business owner have to believe in your business model more than anyone else. You need to have faith in whatever you are doing. If you don't believe yourself, no one else would.

Learning to say "No" is truly a quality that we need to learn in order to stay focused towards our goals.

## Case study: ING Direct

ING direct has built the fastest growing bank in US by adapting to this principle of saying NO. When their customer asks for credit card, their answer is No; when they ask for online brokerage account, their answer is again No.

ING direct wants to keep things simple. That's why the bank offers just a few saving accounts, certificates of deposit, mutual funds and that's it.

Going with limited product features or offerings will help you to scale up your business without adding any cost overheads.

## Steps to build up your retail entrepreneurial venture

There is a wonderful saying "What got you here, won't take you to next level", you need to keep enhancing your skills, keep innovating yourself by breaking old habits ( point of caution- innovation is not always product-centric, it can be very personalized, even the way you think can be innovated)

One important point that I would like to convey to the entrepreneurs is that the VC fund is something like "Vapour Capital" i.e. it evaporates as soon as it comes into your business.

Try to follow the basics of business i.e. if you invest USD 1 into your business, you need to generate USD 2, re-invest this again in your business till your business becomes self-sustaining. If you follow the ratio 1:2, you shall never have cash flow issues in your business.

I am putting down the most important tips which would help upcoming retailpreneurs with their projects.

## 1. Start with your own pain points

The easiest and straightforward way to create a great product or service is to make something you want to use yourself.

As you build the project, you would soon figure out whether or not you are making any good.

## Case study:

Coach Bill Bowerman felt the need for better lighter running shoes for his team. So he went out to his workshop and poured rubber into the family waffle iron. That's how Nike's famous waffle sole was born.

**Key learning:** "Start with your own pain point" and coming out with the solution, lets you fall in love with what you are making.

This very source provides you inner-motivation and go-getter attitude.

## 2. Keep customer focus through-out

Always at the start of any project, keep your customer focused, imagine what you would like your customer to say about your product or service.

## 3. Be Action taker

You should feel urgency about whatever you are planning to start or to do. If you are building a break-through product or service or even a Me-Too product, ***JUST DO IT*** (as Nike says it).

Don't sit around and wait for someone to make the difference that you would like to see.

## Case study

The Drudge Report, run by Matt drudge is just one page on the web run by one guy.

Yet it has a huge impact on the news industry- television, radio talk-show hosts, and newspaper journalists all visit this page daily to find out as to what's trending..

In July 2016, the site garnered 1.47 billion Pageviews, as a result of US Presidential elections

The Drudge Report's traffic beat out the likes of news sites from Disney Media Networks (which includes ESPN.com and ABCNews.com), Yahoo, Google, Time Warner, and Fox Entertainment Groups.

## Key learning

Make the difference that you would like to see yourself. Drudge's report came from nowhere and disrupted the old models that had been around for decades.

## 4. Understand your core "WHY"

Great businesses have a point of view and not just a product or service. You have to believe in something. As you get going, keep in mind as to "why" you are doing "what" you are doing.

Frankly speaking, this is the real Mission and Vision statement of the business.

For instance, Big corporates shell out millions of dollars to copywriters to write it, ideally, it should be written by the founder himself because that is his or her vision.

## Case study

Wholefoods (now a part of amazon.com) stands for selling the highest quality natural and organic products available.

Their customers know and understand Wholefoods purpose, they don't go to their stores asking or looking for potato chips or coke or junk food.

This very "WHY" adds rock-solid positioning for wholefoods and is one of the reasons for their success.

## Key takeaways

The road to entrepreneurship is often a treacherous one filled with unexpected detours, roadblocks and dead ends. There are lots of sleepless nights, plans that don't work out, funding that doesn't come through and customers that never materialize.

It can be so challenging to launch a business that it may make you wonder why anyone willingly sets out on such a path.

Yet despite all these hardships, every year, thousands of entrepreneurs embark on this journey determined to bring their vision to fruition and fulfill a need they see in society. They open brick-and-mortar businesses, launch tech startups, or bring a new product or service into the marketplace.

Most entrepreneurs are spurred on by one or more of the following motivators:-

**Autonomy–** Entrepreneurs want to be their own bosses, set their own goals, control their own progress and run their businesses at how they see it fit.

**Purpose–** Many entrepreneurs have a clear vision of what they want to accomplish and feel compelled to work tirelessly to make that happen. Positive attitude and failing forward are the methodologies that build great entrepreneurs.

No amount of self-help books or courses could help, the entrepreneurs need to build positive attitude and never give up attitude towards life.

# Chapter 11

## Build your own audience

Post running my blog site www.retailritesh.com for over one year and learning about SEO and organic growth of the site, I realized that with the algorithm changes, the traction on social media goes for a toss.

Of late, there is hardly any organic traction that one gets on social channels like Facebook, Instagram etc.

### Social media is changing and that's the fact!!

In a recent survey, 77% percent of brands admitted to using at least one social platform's for their products. Only 48% of marketers admitted that they see ROI from their social media strategy.

**Source:** https://www.smartinsights.com/social-media-marketing/social-media-analytics/social-media-marketing-actually-generate-roi/

If you're one of the brands struggling to see ROI on your social media marketing investment, you won't be surprised when I say this: "Social media *is* changing – and it's not necessarily for the better, at least from a marketing perspective."

## Have you witnessed a drop in your social media engagement recently?

If yes, then the reasons are mentioned below-

Earlier this year, Facebook CEO Mark Zuckerberg announced a huge shift in the way Facebook's News Feed would work.

*"The first changes you'll see will be in News Feed, where you can expect to see more from your friends, family, and groups.*

*As we roll this out, you'll see less public content like posts from businesses, brands, and media".*

## Twitter Is Deleting over a Million Accounts Every Day

With over 70 million suspicious and spam accounts being deleted by the company over the past two months, don't be surprised if you see a significant dip in the number of people following your Twitter profile.

## So why are social media companies doing this?

The answer is simple-They want brands and advertisers to spend on their channels to boost their pages or posts.

Don't be surprised that this move, because this makes all these social media platforms a multi-billion dollar vehicle.

Google is the best example wherein they want you to spend through AdWords to divert traffic onto your website and webpage.

Amazon's biggest traffic comes from AdWords, they are indeed big spenders of dollars on Google.

You would be lucky if your post garnered 3% reach or visibility organically on Facebook or Instagram.

Brands are therefore forced to spend their dollars on to digital advertising by sponsored ads or by AdWords.

## How does this hamper smaller brands and SME's?

- Less reach of their posts or services
- Less organic traction with their followers

So, expect your uphill struggle to boost the organic reach of your business' Facebook posts to continue.

If you're not allocating your cash to the advertising side of Facebook's /Instagram platform, you won't be seen at all.

So it depends on marketers as to how they would like to spend their budgets on social media advertising.

My frank opinion is "Social media is good for generating awareness but one should simultaneously develop their own customized channel of communications and engagement with their customers. That's a more holistic approach".

## Case study: Lush cosmetics.

British cosmetics brand Lush announced in 2019, that it will be quitting several social media platforms in the U.K.

"We are tired of fighting with algorithms, and we do not want to pay to appear in your newsfeed," it said in posts on its Instagram, Twitter, and Facebook accounts.

The company, best known for its colorful bath bombs and soaps, has amassed more than 570,000 Instagram, 200,000 Twitter, and 400,000 Facebook followers.

Points suggested to brands from Lush cosmetics perspective

- Analyze which channel is bringing more traffic to your website.
- Develop your own channels like chatbots, live chats on your website.
- Develop email marketing more holistically.

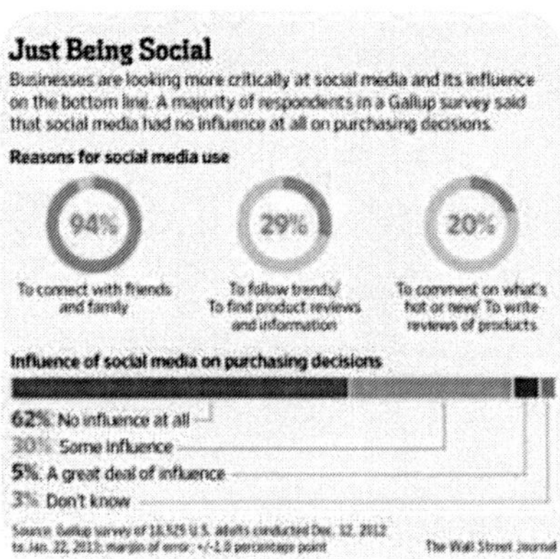


- Explore new platforms like-

House party is an app specifically for live video chatting and co-viewing experiences.

Next door is a network centered on your neighborhood, connecting you with people on the same block.

Yonder focuses on outdoor recreation and lifestyle, allowing for information on people and activities.

These newer alternative platforms may not offer the same reach compared to established players but would be a good start.

# Chapter 12

## Luxury Retailing

Having worked and being involved in leading the team that produced a luxury concept arising from United Arab Emirates (in beauty & fashion domain), I would like to share my wisdom acquired from my personal experience.

Foremost you need to understand the difference between non-luxury brands and luxury brands.

Most non-luxury brands succeed because they are marketed in terms of the problems they solve. These are their reasons for being. For example - Brand X of t-shirt whisks sweat away to keep you cooler A Particular sweetener gives you the taste without the calories, brand car X gets more miles to the gallon so you spend less on over-priced gas.

This is not so much in the business of luxury. No one wears a Burberry trench coat merely to stay warm. No one forks over $200,000 for a Bentley simply to get from point A to point B.

No Luxury products exist for a much less rational reason. Therefore, their marketing must be much more emotional.

In short, mass marketing is the business of selling reality. Luxury marketing is the business of selling dreams.

1. Forget about positioning; luxury is not comparative. Advocate beliefs.

Luxury brands should advocate the beliefs of customers rather than simply rely on brand values. Beliefs go further; they're more specific and, consequently, more segmenting.

Unlike mass brands, luxury brands should not strive to please everyone, but those customers whose beliefs align with their own.

A good example of this is Ferrari's belief in high performance. The brand rarely advertises in mass media, but it invests significant amounts in Formula 1 events. It focuses on actions related to its belief to reinforce this tenet in consumers' minds.

Another good example is Louis Vuitton's belief in art. Among other collaborations, the fashion house linked up with Japanese artist Yayoi Kusama to create a limited edition of products.

In mass markets, brands distribute their investments across several efforts because they want to reach and please the broadest possible spectrum of customers. Instead, luxury brands' investments are focused on the specific beliefs of the brand, creating a much focused experience for the right customers.

2. Bring a sense of exclusivity and experiential emotive

A true luxury brand cannot stop their offering at the product itself; they must go beyond that to offer unique services or rituals. This can start with something as simple as attentive salespeople and prompt customer service, but it should really go beyond that to create a consumption "ritual" that allows customers to experience the brand.

Perfume brand Le Labo does this very well. Using the premise that the quality of perfume deteriorates over time, it revolutionized the consumer buying experience by offering a special personal experience: each Le Labo perfume is hand-blended and individually prepared in front of the customer at the moment of purchase. The glass decanter is then dated and the customer's name is printed on the label. After taking the perfume home, the customer must let it marinate in the fridge for a week before using it. Through this ritual, buying Le Labo perfume becomes more than an exclusive product; it becomes a personal experience.

3. The store becomes the epitome of luxury for discerning customers

Luxury brands must pay extra attention to the way they sell and innovate at the point of purchase. Before, it was enough for luxury brands to use brick and mortar stores to sell their products, but they must now aim to design multifunctional, controlled spaces that create brand experiences and communicate brand beliefs.

BMW World in Munich is another example of a temple-like showroom, where consumers can "experience" the brand rather than simply buy the product.

**BMW world.**

4. Don't respond to the rising demand

One of the key premises that Luxury brands work on is **"Less is more"**. Connoisseurs of luxury brands relish a sense of exclusivity that comes along with Luxury products, its emotional gratification that provides a sense of belonging to the elite club.

One of the most famous and highly successful brands that have mastered this point is Hermes. The bags are scarce, sought-after a simply the best, and they have the price tags that go along with all that exclusivity.

**Hermes- Kelly Bag**

Status… status… status.

If you're looking for a bag to tell everyone who sees you that, not only have you arrived, but you've arrived with exquisite taste, Hermès will do that every single time.

To summarize, I would like to end up with a famous quote by Hubert Givenchy, "Luxury is in each detail".